Animals in the Wild

Kookaburra

by Vincent Serventy

Raintree Childrens Books
Milwaukee • Toronto • Melbourne • London

John Ferguson • Sydney

Kookaburras are Australian kingfishers. The laughing kookaburra is one of the largest of the kingfishers.

It is about one-and-a-half feet long. Its
laughing call can be heard early and late
in the day.

The call tells other kookaburras to stay
away. Kookaburras have other calls that
signal other messages.

The blue-winged kookaburra is almost as big as the laughing kookaburra. The two birds live in different parts of Australia.

Kingfishers and kookaburras can live in rain forests or dry country. They might live along river banks.

Laughing kookaburras nest in holes in trees. If a hole is too small, the bird will use its beak to peck it bigger.

Female kookaburras lay up to four eggs in a nest. Chicks hatch in 25 days. Family members feed the babies.

Chicks can fly in about a month. They are
fed for another month after that. Then they
can take care of themselves.

Kookaburras eat many different kinds of
food. They eat frogs and fish that they hunt
in pools and creeks.

The birds also catch larger animals like
snakes. A kookaburra will beat its prey
against a log or rock until it is soft.

Once a snake has been beaten, it can be eaten. Kookaburras can eat snakes that are over three feet long.

If the snake is too long, the kookaburra
has to stop to rest for a while. Then it will
be able to swallow more.

Some snakes are poisonous. Kookaburras
hold them by the head. That way the
snakes cannot bite.

Kookaburras stay in the same place the
whole year. Sometimes there are five or six
birds in a family group.

There are enemies. One of them is the
goshawk. It hunts from the air and swoops
down to kill other birds.

There are dangers from the ground, too.
Pet cats hunt many garden birds. They
climb trees and attack nests.

Kookaburras might live near towns and cities. They can become tame. They like to eat cheese and pieces of meat.

The kookaburras are most common in the Australian forests. There they have plenty of food.

First published in the United States of America 1985
by Raintree Publishers Inc., 330 East Kilbourn Avenue,
Milwaukee, Wisconsin 53202.

Library of Congress Number 84-17969

First published in Australia in 1983
by John Ferguson Pty. Ltd.
133 Macquarie Street
Sydney, NSW, 2000

Acknowledgements are due to Vincent Serventy
for all photographs in this book except the following:
Graham D. Anderson p. 8; Ray Garston p. 9; David Hollands p. 20;
Ralph & Daphne Keller p. 5, 6-7; Harold Pollack p. 12, 13;
W.R. Taylor p. 10; A.D. & M.C. Trounson pp. 14-15;
Eric Worrell p. 16, 17.

ISBN 0-8172-2417-3 (U.S.A.)

Library of Congress Cataloging in Publication Data

Serventy, Vincent.
      Kookaburra.

      (Animals in the wild)
      Summary: Shows the kookaburra in its natural surround-
ings and describes its life and struggles for survival.
         1. Kookaburra—Juvenile literature. [1. Kookaburra]
I. Title. II. Series.
QL696.C72S47 1985   598.8′92   84-17969
ISBN 0-8172-2417-3

1234567890   89 88 87 86 85